JIMMY'S JOKE BOOK

First published in 1997 by
Mercier Press
PO Box 5, 5 French Church Street Cork
16 Hume Street Dublin 2
Trade enquiries to CMD Distribution
55A Spruce Avenue
Stillorgan Industrial Park
Blackrock County Dublin

ISBN 1 85635 203 X

10 9 8 7 6 5 4 3 2 1

A CIP record for this title is available
from the British Library

Cover design by Penhouse Design
Set by Richard Parfrey
Printed in Ireland by ColourBooks
Baldoyle Industrial Estate, Dublin 13

JIMMY'S JOKE BOOK

MERCIER PRESS

FOREWORD

Ten years ago I answered my studio on-air phone to a funny guy with a funny voice, who had obviously dialled a wrong number. He was actually looking for a pest-control company. After speaking to him for over an hour, so was I.

To be honest, he made me laugh with his light-hearted approach to life and his remarkable ability to tell a good story, so I decided to put him on air.

Listeners obviously liked what they heard too, because the *Breakfast Show* desk in 2FM was inundated with requests to have him back on. And that is how 'Jimmy' began.

Soon after, it became clear that he wasn't going away, and I've been stuck with him ever since!

Sometimes we have a chuckle over everyday things and other times a real belly laugh. Either way, I am convinced, and so too is the programme's producer John 'Victor' Clarke, that the world is a better place with Jimmy in it.

We've had some great times together, and lots of fun. Trips abroad are particularly memorable. Over the years, Jimmy has become a good friend, and like all good friends he's always there when he needs you.

Then, of course, there are Jimmy's friends: Maurice the chancer, zero-personality Plunket, clumsy Mr Bolger and 'outside NOW!' Drayfus. And how could we dare forget his beautiful wife, Violet 'Violence' Mooney. Some woman for one woman.

Jimmy's keen observation of human life and behaviour,

together with his quick wit, has made him an institution on Irish radio; so much so that his many catchphrases, like 'Get outta dat garden', 'Go on outta dat' and, in relation to some of his cornier jokes, 'Keep throwin' them out – you can throw that one out for a start!' are now used in everyday conversation.

For a long time now, I, along with many others, have been suggesting that he write a book. He says he will, but first he wants to make some money from a joke book!

So here we are, over ten years and four thousand phone calls later (sorry, RTÉ, the reverse charges were his idea), much to the delight of many, he has finally got it together.

Jimmy's Joke Book – a must-have collection of great gags, funny stories and one-liners, that will leave you wanting more. But you'll have to wait; the real Jimmy book is on the way.

Get outta dat garden, Roddy Doyle!

Ian Dempsey, 2FM

ACKNOWLEDGEMENTS

My thanks to:

Ian, for laughing, even when you didn't have to, John Clarke for guidance and Deirdre Magee for almost four thousand wake-up calls. A great team, and great friends.

My thanks also to Bill O'Donovan for words of encouragement. 'My office, NOW!'

And special thanks to Brendan, Gerry, Gay and Dustin, and all in 2FM.

In particular, my grateful thanks to all the loyal 'Jimmy' fans, and a special girl who really makes me laugh.

Jimmy

A woman goes in to see her doctor.

'I'm not feeling very well, doctor, I'm very chesty. Do you think you'll be able to help?'

'Oh, I think I'll be able to help all right. Tell me this, are you getting a little tickle in the mornings?'

'Well, doctor,' says she, 'I used to, but not since they changed the milkman.'

An old lady is sitting in a restaurant, enjoying a cup of tea. She can't help but notice the waiter, who is busy scratching his backside furiously.

She calls him over. 'Excuse me, love, but do you have haemorrhoids?'

The waiter says, 'No, missus, I'm sorry, only what it says on the menu.'

An old man goes into a chip shop and says to the girl behind the counter, 'Excuse me, love, could I have a bag of chips please?'

'Certainly,' says the girl. 'Eighty-five or ninety-five?'

'Ah,' says your man, 'if you're going to start countin' them, forget it.'

A fella goes into Superquinn and heads straight for the frozen foods department. Looking around nervously, he grabs a frozen chicken and makes a dash for the door.

The security man spots him and shouts, 'Oi, what are doing with that chicken?'

Quick as a flash your man shouts back, 'Well, I was going to do some roast potatoes and a nice bit of broccoli.'

An elderly man goes to see his doctor.

'Tell me this, doc, and give it to me straight. Do you think I'll live till I'm ninety?'

'Well,' says the doctor, 'how old are you now?'

'Seventy-seven,' says the man.

'And tell me this,' says the doc, 'do you smoke?'

'No,' says the man.

'Do you take a drink at all?'

'No,' says the man.

'Do you ever back the odd horse?'

'No, doctor, never.'

'Well, tell me this, do you ever stay out late dancing, or chasing a bit of the quare thing at all?'

'No,' says the man.

'Then,' says the doctor, 'what the bloody hell do you want to live till you're ninety for?'

An American tourist is standing on O'Connell Bridge, looking up at Liberty Hall. He notices someone leaning over the edge, and then falling off.

He rushes down the quays and discovers a man lying on the ground, and there's blood everywhere. Offering the injured man his coat to use as a pillow, the Yank enquires, 'What the hell happened?'

'I haven't got a clue,' says your man. 'I'm only after getting here myself.'

A man rushes into a garda station.

'Help, help, guard, you've got to help me.'

'What's the matter?' asks the duty officer.

'It's my mother-in-law, she's just tried to run me over in her car.'

'And how do you know it's your mother-in-law?' enquires the officer.

Your man says, 'I'd recognise that laugh anywhere.'

A man walks into a chemist's shop.

'Excuse me,' he says to the assistant, 'but do you examine bottoms here?'

'We do,' says the assistant.

'Well,' says your man, 'would you mind washing your hands, and giving us a half-pound of cough drops.'

Mother-in-law was ill in bed, when the doctor came. Placing a thermometer in her mouth, the doctor says, 'Don't open your mouth for fifteen minutes.'

Afterwards the son-in-law took the doctor aside and whispered, 'Look, doc, how much do you want for that thing?'

I was travelling on the bus the other day when the bus conductor says, 'You've had a row with your mother-in-law, haven't you?'

'How the hell did you know that?' I asked.

'Well,' says your man, 'you've still got the axe stuck in your head.'

Two golfers were out on the course together, and one of them seemed to be taking an extraordinary amount of time and trouble with his next drive. His companion asked him why.

'Well,' says the golfer, 'I'm very anxious to make this shot a good one. My mother-in-law came to the course with me today and she's up in the clubhouse watching me.'

'Don't be ridiculous,' says his friend. 'You haven't a hope of hitting her from here.'

The man who invented cat's-eyes
Apparently this man was walking along a lonely country road late one night, when he stumbled and fell. As he was getting up he noticed two little green lights in front of him.

He was puzzled at first, but then realised it was only a cat. He thought that this could be of great benefit to drivers, so he invented and perfected the cat's-eyes.

Mind you, if the cat had been facing the other way, he would have invented the pencil sharpener!

A couple are asleep in bed one night, when the wife is woken by noises.

So she wakes the husband, who isn't too pleased.

'There's someone downstairs,' she whispers, 'and I can hear him eating that casserole I made for tomorrow night.'

'Don't worry,' says the husband, 'sure go back to sleep now and I'll call the doctor for him first thing in the morning.'

Two women are talking over the garden wall.

'Hey,' says one of them, 'What do you think of our son Kevin? He's after taking up meditating, for hours on end.'

'Well,' says the other woman, 'I suppose it's better than him sitting around all day doing nothing.'

There was a break-out from the lunatic asylum in Cavan.

So the local gardaí called in the army, the fire brigade and the villagers to help them find the patients. They had great success and at the end of the day had managed to round up forty-five.

The problem was, only fifteen had escaped.

Did you hear about the doctor who turned kidnapper, but failed because no-one could read his ransom note?

A man is up before a judge in America for a divorce.

The judge says to him, 'All right, sir, please tell me why you want a divorce.'

'Because,' says the man, 'I live in a two-storey house.'

'You live in a two-storey house?' says the judge. 'What kind of reason is that for a divorce?'

'Well,' says your man, 'one story is "I have a headache" and the other story is "I'm very tired".'

A man goes to the doctor, suffering from a bad case of memory loss.

'You'll have to help me, doctor, I keep forgetting things. What can I do?'

'Well,' says the doc, 'you can pay me in advance for a start.'

A fella walks into the chemist's and says, 'Excuse me, do you have any talcum powder?'

'Certainly,' says the chemist. 'Walk this way.'

Your man says, 'If I could walk that way, I wouldn't need the talcum powder.'

This guy goes to the doctor and says, 'Doc, I've had a fifty-pence piece stuck in my ear for months.'

The doctor says, 'Why didn't you come to see me sooner?'

'Well,' says your man, 'I didn't need the money.'

A psychiatrist says to his patient, 'I want to congratulate you on the progress you've been making.'

The patient replies, 'Progress? What progress? Six months ago I was Napoleon, and today I'm nobody. And you call that progress?'

Fella goes to the doctor. Says he, 'I'm not feeling very well.'

So the doctor examines him and says, 'I'm sorry, Mr Murphy, but I can't do anything. I'm afraid your complaint is hereditary.'

'Well,' says your man, 'you can send my father the bill.'

Christmas morning, and the young kid is playing with his chemistry set.

The father says, 'If you touch that red bottle one more time you're going upstairs.'

And the kid says, 'Dad, if you touch me, we're both going upstairs.'

A Polish guy goes to the optician.

The optician says, 'Can you read all those letters there?'

And the Polish guy says, 'Read them? I went to school with half of them.'

A Scottish chap, over for the rugby weekend, goes into Switzers and says to the assistant, 'I want to buy my wife a really nice present for her birthday, perhaps some perfume.'

'Ah,' says the salesgirl, 'that will be a nice surprise for her.'

'It certainly will,' says your man. 'She's expecting a fur coat.'

A friend of mine says to me the other night he has to go over to the Phoenix Park to tell his elderly mother – who's riding in the six-day cycle race – some bad news.

I says to him, 'Don't be silly, the six-day cycle race finished three days ago.'

He says, 'I know, that's what I want to tell her.'

If it takes three Irishmen to change a light bulb – one to hold the bulb, and two of them to turn the room – and it takes four Californians – one to change it, and three to share the experience – how many Jewish mothers does it take to change a light bulb?

None.

'Don't worry about me, I'll just sit here in the dark.'

When I see all the new clothes the children are wearing these days, it makes me wonder.

I used to get all my father's cast-offs.

In particular I used to hate getting his old trousers.

I had to pull down the fly just to blow my nose.

My mother used to buy our clothes secondhand, in the army and navy store in Dublin.

It wasn't easy going to school at age five, dressed as a Japanese admiral.

An elderly couple are sitting on the couch watching TV.

Suddenly there's a gas explosion and the two of them are catapulted through the roof and land in the front garden.

Someone calls an ambulance and it soon arrives. The couple are dusting themselves down when the ambulance-man enquires, 'Are you both OK?'

'Oh, I feel fine,' says the lady. 'In fact, it's the first time we've been out together in twenty-five years.'

I met this woman the other day at the shops and we got talking. She told me that she had twenty-two children.

'My God,' I says, 'twenty-two children. You must love them a lot.'

'Love them!' she says. 'Jesus, I don't even know half of them.'

The husband had his suspicions about his cheating wife. In fact, he knew she was having an affair. One night he was out for a walk in the local park, and as he strolled along, who does he see but his wife, cuddling up to a man on the park bench.

He shouts over to her, 'Why you . . . why you . . . Now I know everything.'

'Oh yeah?' she shouts back. 'Well, what year was the Battle of the Boyne then?'

Two men are having a chat over a pint. One of them says, 'Des, do you believe in reincarnation?'

After a short silence Des replies, 'Can I get back to you on that?'

Did you hear about the Australian guy who got a new boomerang?

It took him a month to throw away the old one.

A couple arrive at their hotel for a weekend break. They don't know that there is a ballet going on at the same venue. The lady says to the receptionist, 'We'd like to check in, please.'

'Certainly,' says the receptionist. '*The Nutcracker Suite*?'

'No,' says the husband, 'just an ordinary room, please.'

A fella told me a story once about his mother-in-law, who went to Australia for a holiday. While she was there she decided to go swimming. She was enjoying herself until she was attacked by a great white shark.

Apparently the doctors worked hard all through the night, but it was no good. The poor old shark died in the end.

A fella goes to the doctor.

'Doctor, you'll have to help me, I keep thinking I'm a dog.'

'Fair enough,' says the doc, 'sit up there on the couch and I'll have a look at you.'

'No,' says your man, 'I'm not allowed on the couch.'

I'm down at our local fire station one day having a look around.

I see all these big strong firemen being put through their paces. I can't help but notice over in a corner one of them who was only about four foot tall.

I says to the officer in charge, 'Is he any good?'

'Oh, he is,' says the officer, 'but we only use him for small fires.'

An Irishman is being given a tour of the *Mary Rose*, the famous English warship.

'And this,' says the guide, pointing to a brass plate on the deck, 'is where the gallant captain fell.'

'I'm not surprised,' says the Irishman, 'I nearly slipped on it myself.'

A fella goes to the doctor.

'Doctor, you've got to help me, I think I've got double vision.'

'No problem,' says the doc. 'Sit down there on the couch and I'll have a look at you.'

And your man says, 'Sorry, doctor, which one?'

A chap goes to the optician and explains that he keeps seeing spots in front of his eyes. So the optician examines him and gives him a new pair of glasses to try.

'How are they?' he asks. 'Do they help?'

'Well, yeah, sort of,' says the man. 'I can see the spots much clearer now.'

Did you hear about the Irishman doing his first bank robbery?

The manager convinced him to take a cheque, because it might be dangerous carrying all that cash around.

An American tourist is going through the Amazon jungle one day.

In a clearing he comes across a huge dead elephant, with a little pygmy standing beside it.

'My God,' says the American, 'is that elephant dead?'

'It certainly is,' says the pygmy.

'And who killed it?' enquires the Yank.

'I did,' says the pygmy.

'You killed it? Don't be ridiculous. How could a little thing like you kill a massive creature like that elephant?'

'I killed him with a club,' came the reply.

'Well, it must be a very big club,' says the American.

'Oh, it certainly is,' says the pygmy. 'There's nearly three hundred of us in it now.'

Fella goes to the doctor.

'Well, Mr Murphy, how did you get on with those tablets I gave you to improve your memory?'

And Murphy replies, 'What tablets?'

This fella goes into a pub and he has a giraffe with him.

So he sits up at a stool and the giraffe does likewise.

The man orders a whiskey for himself and a gin and tonic for the giraffe.

They knock them back and order the same again.

Two hours later the pair of them are langered. The giraffe is leaning back to knock back his last drink, when he collapses off the stool.

With that, the man starts to head for the door.

'Oi!' shouts the barman. 'You can't leave that lyin' there.'

The drunk turns around, focuses on the barman and slurs, 'It's not a lion, it's a giraffe!'

Maurice and Vera go to a fashion show one night. All the latest lingerie and beachwear are being displayed by tall, leggy, beautiful models.

'My God,' says Vera, 'that's shameful. I don't mind telling you, if I looked like that, I'd never leave the bedroom.'

'Jaysus, Vera,' says Maurice, 'if you looked like that, neither would I.'

I never realised just how much of a stimulant coffee was until some time ago, when a friend of mine who drank fifteen cups a day dropped dead. And three days later he was still mingling at the funeral.

A man phones his doctor one day.

'Doctor, you'll have to help me, I think I'm suffering from incontinence.'

The doctor says, 'Certainly I'll help. Where are you ringing from?'

And your man says, 'From the waist down.'

Slavemaster to galley slaves: 'First the good news. You can all have fifteen minutes' rest from rowing. Now the bad news. After that, the captain wants to go water-skiing.'

A friend of mine was telling me that his wife had died last Sunday week and that he hadn't buried her until the Sunday just gone.

'God, Pat,' says I, 'that's a bit strange.'

'I know, Jimmy,' says he, 'but I always promised her a quiet week with just the two of us.'

A fella walks up to me in the street one day and says, 'Hey, pal, would you have £15.50 for a cup of coffee?'

I says to him, 'Why do you need £15.50?'

He says, 'Well, I hate the taste of coffee, so I want to wash it down with a bottle of Scotch.'

A gamekeeper was walking across his land one day when he spotted a naked lady walking towards him.

'Are you game?' he shouted.

'I am,' came the reply.

So he shot her.

A man says to the waiter in a restaurant one evening, 'I think I'll have a dozen oysters.'

The waiter says, 'But oysters aren't at their peak at the moment, sir.'

'Neither am I,' says the man. 'That's why I want a dozen oysters.'

Prison warden to prisoner: 'And what do you want to see the governor for?'
Prisoner: 'Well, I've been here for eleven months now and I still haven't heard a word about holidays.'

Two fellas are talking in a pub. One says, 'I took my dog to the vet today because it bit my wife.'

His friend asks, 'Did you have him put to sleep?'

'I did not,' says the fella. 'I had his teeth sharpened.'

Goldilocks with a few drinks on her: 'OK, who's been sleeping in my porridge?'

Mr O'Leary was fed up with his wife's insistence on absolute neatness.

He wasn't allowed to smoke cigarettes or cigars or even his beloved pipe at home. He had to take his shoes off before he entered the house and his fussy wife even made him comb his hair in the garden in case he got any dandruff on the carpet.

But when he died Mr O'Leary managed to get some revenge. His last will and testament stated that his ashes were to be scattered all over the living-room floor!

The boss says to his secretary, 'I just don't know what to do. I'm in a real dilemma. What can I give to a valued client – a man who has expensive cars, an art collection worth millions? He has homes in Paris, Switzerland and Hong Kong. In fact, he's a man who has just about everything. What can I give him?'

The secretary looks at him and says, 'You can give him my phone number.'

A woman is walking in Stephen's Green one day with eleven children following her.

'Good afternoon,' calls a friendly gardener. 'Are all the children yours, or is it a picnic?'

'Unfortunately,' says the woman, 'the children are all mine, and believe me, it's certainly no picnic.'

A woman goes to the doctor.

'I'm very concerned, doctor.'

'What's the matter?' says the doc. 'What are you concerned about?'

'Well,' says the woman, 'it's my son. He's always playing with dolls.'

'Oh,' says the doctor, 'I wouldn't worry too much about that.'

'I'm not worried,' says the woman, 'but his wife is very upset.'

This old Morris Minor pulls up outside a pub in a small village one day.

It is in bits, covered in dents and scratches, the paintwork is terrible and all the tyres are bald. There is steam pouring out of the engine and even the nodding dog on the back window has fleas.

The driver gets out and says to a local, sitting outside the pub, 'Would you mind keeping an eye on the car for me while I make a phone call?'

The local agrees and when the driver returns five minutes later he says, 'That will be ten pounds, please.'

'What!' says the driver. 'Ten pounds, just for looking after my car for a few minutes. That's disgraceful!'

'It wasn't the time involved,' says the local, 'it was the embarrassment. Everyone thought it was my car.'

This priest stops a man walking down the street with a roll of cloth under his arm.

'Where did you get that?' asks the priest.

'I robbed it,' says the man.

'Well,' says the priest, 'I hope you're not going to make a habit of it.'

'No,' says your man, 'I'm going to make a sports jacket.'

A Scotsman, an Englishman and a Jew have a six-course meal at a very expensive restaurant.

When the waiter presents them with a bill for £180, the Scotsman says, 'I'll get that.'

The headline in next day's paper reads: 'Jewish ventriloquist found dead in laneway'.

A soccer fan is sitting in the corner of the local pub crying into his beer.

Just then his pal walks in. 'What's the matter with you, Mick?'

'You might well ask me what's wrong, you might well ask,' says the whinger.

'What's wrong then?' asks the pal.

'You won't believe me,' comes the reply, 'you won't believe me.'

'Try me,' says the friend.

'Well, I've been doing nights for the past four years, and I've just discovered the wife is seeing another man. The two kids have run off to England. When I got home from work this morning I discovered the house had burned down with all my possessions in it ... and on top of all that, Liverpool lost three–one.'

'Ah, come on,' says the friend. 'Don't upset yourself.'

'Upset myself?' sobs your man. 'I can't understand it. They were winning at half-time.'

This gamekeeper goes to Africa with his wife and his mother-in-law. They hire a guide who takes them into the wilds of the jungle. One night the husband and wife wake and discover that the mother-in-law is missing. They wake the guide and go looking for her.

Eventually, after an hour searching for her, they find her in a clearing, with a huge lion standing beside her.

'Oh my God,' says the wife, 'what are we going to do?'

'Well,' says the husband, 'the lion got himself into this fix, now let him get out of it.'

An old tortoise was making his way down a laneway late one night. Two snails were waiting in the shadows and when he passed they jumped him and mugged him.

He woke up the next day in hospital.

'You were very lucky,' says the doctor. 'It was touch and go there for a while. In fact we nearly lost you. What the hell happened anyway?'

'I don't know,' says the tortoise. 'It all happened so fast.'

A fella goes to the doctor and explains that every time he drinks a cup of tea he gets a very sharp pain in his left eye. The doctor examines him and says, 'Have you tried taking the spoon out of the cup?'

Murphy is walking down the village one day, looking very angry.

An American tourist stops him and asks what is the matter.

'Well,' says Murphy, 'I was in the local pub just now, and an Englishman says that the Irish are always fighting and causing trouble wherever they go. And I says, "That's a big lie."'

'What happened then?' asks the American.

'Well,' says Murphy, 'I wrecked the place.'

A doddery old man sent a postcard to his local doctor. It read: 'Having a wonderful time. The weather is terrific and the food couldn't be better. Where am I?'

I heard a young boy say to his mother at a sale-of-work one day, 'Mammy, will I buy a big book to put under the kitchen table to stop it wobbling?'

The mother says, 'Yeah, and while you're at it, get one for your father.'

Did you hear about the three-foot guy who was thrown out of a nudist camp in France?

He kept sticking his nose into people's private business.

A bachelor company executive was in with the taxman, filling in his returns.

The taxman was going over the finer details of his account, when suddenly he raised his head and says, 'This is odd, you being a bachelor and claiming tax relief for a dependant son. It must have been a typist's error.'

'It certainly was,' says your man. 'She told me it was safe.'

A magician was being interviewed on television about the secrets of magic.

'What's your favourite trick?' asked the interviewer.

'Sawing a woman in half,' came the reply.

'And tell me this,' says the interviewer, 'do you have any brothers or sisters?'

'Well,' says the magician, 'I have six half-sisters.'

Doctor, doctor, my wife thinks she's a duck.'

'Well, bring her in to see me straight away,' says the doc.

'I can't,' says the man. 'She's already flown south for the winter.'

A missionary went to a remote part of the world to teach and spread the good word to the natives. On his travels he came to a small village, where he decided to make a speech. It went something like this.

'All men are your enemies, and you must love your enemies.'

The natives all raised their spears and shouted in unison, 'Mussanga.'

The missionary continued, 'If a man should insult you, you should turn the other cheek.'

Again the natives responded with 'Mussanga.'

'Fighting is wrong, God does not like it, so you should put aside all your anger.'

Yet again the natives raised their spears and roared, 'Mussanga.'

Then the missionary decided that he had talked enough for one day, so, still on the platform, he turned to the native nearest to him and says, 'I think my little speech went down quite well, don't you? They all seemed to agree with what I had to say. What do you think?'

'Oh, eh, I don't know,' says the native. 'Just watch yourself getting down there, that you don't step in any of that ol' mussanga.'

Ad seen in *Stage* magazine: 'Human cannonball wanted for circus. Must be prepared to travel long distances. Only men of highest calibre should apply.'

A man goes into a clothes shop and says to the assistant, 'I'd like to try on that suit in the window.'

'I'm sorry,' says the assistant. 'You'll have to use the changing room like everyone else.'

A Dublin Corporation worker was walking along O'Connell Street, kicking a tortoise. A garda was watching this for a while, and decided to investigate.

'Hold on there,' he says. 'Why are you kicking that poor defenceless tortoise?'

The Corporation worker paused for a moment and says, 'Because he's been following me around all day.'

A fella was telling me the one about the two elephants that were walking down Henry Street. One of the elephants told the other that he wanted to fart.

'Oh, but you can't do it here,' says the other elephant. 'It will make far too much noise. You'll have to go and do it up in the Phoenix Park.'

The fella says to me then, 'Did you hear it?'

'No,' says I.

'Well, you would have,' says he, 'if you'd been up in the Phoenix Park.'

A one-armed man goes to the barber's shop for a shave.

The barber begins, and within a few minutes he's cut the customer about ten times with the open razor. There's blood everywhere.

To make conversation, the barber says, 'Have I shaved you before?'

'No,' says the customer, 'I lost the arm in the war.'

A man took his dog to the pictures with him to see *Watership Down*.

The manager was just about to approach the man to ask him to leave, but then realised that the dog appeared to be enjoying himself.

When the movie was over and the man and his dog were leaving, the manager says, 'I was very surprised to see that your dog really enjoyed the film.'

'So was I,' says the man. 'He didn't like the book at all.'

Two little boys are looking around an art gallery. They come across an expensive painting, which is extremely abstract. One of the boys says to the other, 'Quick, let's get out of here before they think we did it.'

Piano tuner: 'Good afternoon, Mrs Murphy, I've come to tune your piano.'
Mrs Murphy: 'But I didn't ask for a piano tuner to call.'
Piano Tuner: 'I know, Mrs Murphy, but your neighbours did.'

A husband and wife are chatting.

'I don't think I like this bananas-only diet the doctor has me on,' says the wife. 'It seems to be having a strange effect on me.'

'Don't be silly,' says the husband. 'Now will you stop scratching yourself and come down from those curtains.'

A policeman saw an elderly man pulling a cardboard box along the street on a lead.

'God love him,' thought the policeman, 'I'd better humour him.'

'That's a fine looking dog you have there,' he says to the man.

'It's not a dog, it's a box,' replied the man.

'Oh,' says the policeman, walking away, 'I'm terribly sorry, I just thought you were a bit simple.'

The man turned and winked at the box. 'We fooled him that time, didn't we, Rover?'

Maurice and Vera go on a holiday to the Holy Land, and naturally visit the Sea of Galilee.

They see a local boatman and approach him. 'Can you take us across the lake?'

'No problem,' says the boatman, 'that will be twenty pounds each.'

'Twenty pounds each?' says Maurice. 'That's an awful lot of money.'

'I know,' says the boatman, 'but don't forget, the good Lord himself walked across these waters.'

'Well,' says Maurice, 'at twenty quid a head for the boat, I'm not surprised he walked.'

A man goes to see his doctor.

'Doctor,' says he, 'you'll have to help me. I have this mole on my chest, and whenever women see it they go wild with passion and they can't seem to keep their hands off me. Can you give me anything for it?'

Quick as a flash the doctor replies, 'I'll give you my BMW.'

A woman went to an animal auction to purchase a parrot.

She was bidding furiously for fifteen minutes. At last her bid was successful and she went to pay the auctioneer.

'I assume this bird can talk,' she says.

'Talk?' says the auctioneer. 'Who the hell do you think has been bidding against you for the last quarter of an hour?'

A Scottish tourist ran out of petrol in a small Irish village, opposite the local pub.

There was a local sitting outside having a pint, so the Scotsman asked him if he would mind giving him a push to the garage, which was about three hundred yards away.

Rather reluctantly the local agreed and, with a great amount of effort, pushed the car to the petrol pump. By the time he reached the garage he was totally out of breath.

The Scotsman, who had remained in the car, asked for ten pounds' worth of petrol.

When the tank was full he gave the attendant ten pounds and then searched in his pockets for some small change for the man who had pushed his car.

After a moment he discovered that he had no change on him, so he wound down his window and says to the local, 'I'm very sorry, but I've just spent all my money on petrol, so I can't tip you. Do you smoke, by any chance?'

The local, still out of breath, replied, 'Yes, as a matter of fact I do.'

'Well,' says the Scotsman, 'if I were you, I'd give them up, because you look knackered.'

The judge was cross-eyed, and three men were up before him for robbing.

He says to the first man, 'Well, how do you plead, guilty or not guilty?'

The second man says, 'Not guilty.'

The judge says, 'I wasn't talking to you.'

And the third fella says, 'I didn't open my mouth.'

An American tourist was on holiday in Ireland.

Feeling quite thirsty he walked into Mulligan's bar. There was no one there except Mulligan himself.

He says to the tourist, 'I'm sorry, sir, I can't serve you. We don't open for another hour, but you're welcome to sit here and wait.'

The American says, 'That's very kind of you.' And he sat down in a corner with his newspaper.

A few minutes later Mulligan came over to him and says, 'Would you like a drink while you're waiting?'

A Scotsman was on holiday in Dublin and staying at a big hotel.

He was only there two days, and he had a complaint to make about some of the other guests, so he went to see the manager.

'What seems to be the problem?' enquired the friendly manager.

'Well, it's like this,' says the Scotsman. 'At around four o'clock every morning the other guests are hammering on my bedroom door. They're banging on the walls, they're banging on the ceiling and they're even shouting obscenities. Sometimes the noise is so bad I can't even hear myself playing my bagpipes.'

A leading celebrity with a serious drink problem was asked to launch a ship.

It took him three days. He wouldn't let go of the bottle.

A drunk was staggering home from the pub one night, wondering how he could hide his condition from his wife. Eventually he decided that when he got home he'd sit in the parlour and read a book. His wife would be impressed and wouldn't suspect him of being drunk if he was reading.

He finally arrived home and sneaked into the parlour and sat down.

A few minutes later his wife came storming into the room. 'And what the hell do you think you're doing?' she shouted.

'Just reading, darling, just reading,' came the casual reply.

'You're not, you're bloody drunk again,' she fumed. 'Now close that suitcase and get up to bed.'

A family was visiting the Chamber of Horrors at Madame Tussaud's in London.

An attendant approached the father and pointed to a woman who was standing still, staring at a very frightening and gruesome exhibit. 'Excuse me, sir, but is that lady with you?'

'She is,' says the man. 'That's the mother-in-law.'

'Well,' says the attendant, 'will you ask her to keep moving? We're stocktaking today.'

A man was working late one night. So late in fact that he missed the last train home and had to walk fifteen miles. Eventually he arrived home around five in the morning and was puzzled to see all the lights on and his wife standing at the door looking very distressed.

'Oh, thank God you're back,' she says, giving him a big hug. 'We've had a burglar in our bedroom.'

'Did he get anything?' asked the anxious husband.

'He certainly did,' says the wife. 'I thought it was you.'

Maurice and Vera are sitting by the fire one evening, relaxing and enjoying the company of their faithful dog, Rover.

Vera says, 'I think Rover is getting on a bit.'

'Why do you say that?' asks Maurice.

'Well, I think he's going a bit deaf.'

'Nonsense!' says Maurice. 'Watch this.'

Maurice looks over at the dog and says, 'Sit, Rover, sit!'

A few seconds later Maurice turns to Vera and with a sheepish grin says, 'I think you're right, love. I'll get a shovel and clean it up.'

An enthusiastic young actor heard that a big theatre in the city was looking for some fresh talent. In particular, they were searching for someone who could convincingly play the part of the late president of America, John F. Kennedy.

Very determined, the young actor set about studying his subject. He read everything he could about the late president. He learned about his mannerisms and habits, and he even went as far as taking speech lessons so he could imitate JFK perfectly. On top of all this, he discovered an excellent make-up artist, who, on the day of the auditions, made him up in such a way that he bore an amazing resemblance to the late president.

Unfortunately he didn't get the part.

But he was assassinated on his way home.

Maurice is out of work.

One day in his local pub he overhears some guy mention that a nearby manufacturing company is looking for a chief accountant. Having been out of work for so long, he's desperate, so he applies for the job.

Amazingly, he gets a call and is invited to do a first interview. It goes fine.

Two weeks later, another phone call, and a second interview. It goes great.

A month later the phone rings again. Can he attend a third interview? He can't believe his luck. He turns up and sails through it.

Next morning he receives a telegram marked *Urgent*, requesting him to be in the company's head office at three o'clock that very afternoon.

Maurice puts on his best suit and presents himself, as requested, at three o'clock precisely. The chief executive greets him and introduces him to the board.

'Well, Maurice,' begins the chairman, 'I think we've found the right man for the job. From the moment we first met you, you have impressed us all. As you know, we are an international company, with overseas offices and a workforce of almost twenty thousand. Your job will be a demanding one, handling all the financial dealings, all the investments, all the salaries, and, of course, all our daily dealings with the banks.

'Your remuneration will, of course, reflect the importance of the position.

'I would now like officially to offer you the position of chief accountant, company car included, and a salary of forty-seven thousand pounds a year. How does that sound?'

'It sounds terrific,' says Maurice. 'How much does that work out at a week?'

A man is at a football match enjoying the game, but his attention is distracted by the man next to him who has a dog with him.

Every time United score, the dog jumps up in the air, claps his paws together, gives a gasping laugh and settles back into his seat.

The man is amazed.

Half-time arrives and, as everyone heads for some refreshments, the keen football fan turns to the man with the dog.

'That's some dog you have there,' he says.

'Don't be talking,' comes the quiet reply.

'I'm sorry to appear forward,' says the keen football fan, 'but I couldn't help noticing that every time United scored, your dog jumped in the air, clapped his paws together and gave a gasping laugh. What does he do if your team is losing?'

'Oh, he does somersaults,' came the reply.

'And how many somersaults would he do?' enquired the football fan.

'Oh,' says the man, 'that depends on how hard I kick him up the arse.'

A motorist was stopped by a motorcycle garda, who informed him that he was speeding.

'I most certainly was not,' retorted the motorist. 'The most I was doing was fifty.'

'I'm afraid,' says the garda, 'you were doing eighty-five.'

'Nothing of the sort, I tell you I was only doing fifty,' the motorist replied angrily.

'There's no use arguing with him, guard,' the driver's wife interjected. 'He's always like this when he's had a few drinks.'

Customer in restaurant: 'Excuse me, but do you have any wild duck?'

Waiter: 'No, sir, I'm afraid not, but we do have a tame one that we could irritate for you.'

A patient goes to see his doctor because he has formed a nasty habit of stealing.

'Well now, Mr Smith, what I want you to do is take three of these tablets every day for a fortnight.'

'And what if that doesn't work?' enquired the patient.

'Well, in that case,' says the doctor, 'would you mind getting me a case of Scotch, a video camera and a colour television?'

A cowboy walks into a saloon, slams his fist on the bar and shouts, 'Whiskey.'

He drinks the whiskey, whips out his Colt 45 and shoots a nick in the ear lobe of the piano player.

'More whiskey,' he shouts, and as the barman is serving him, he advises the cowboy that he should file the sights off the gun. So he files them off and orders another whiskey. He knocks it back, turns around and shoots the pianist's hat off.

'More whiskey,' he shouts.

The nervous-looking barman serves him and suggests to the cowboy that he might like to grease the barrel. In fact the barman insists, 'It'll be much better if you grease the barrel.'

'How the hell,' says the cowboy, 'will it be much better if I file off the sights and grease the barrel?'

'Because,' says the barman, 'when Wyatt Earp is finished playing that piano, he's gonna shove that gun right up your arse.'

A little boy was kneeling by the bedside when his father came in to say goodnight. Seeing his son apparently saying his prayers, the father knelt down on the other side of the bed.

'Hiya, Dad,' says the little boy. 'What are you doing?'

The father lowered his head and says, 'Just the same as you, my son, just the same as you.'

'Well, I wouldn't if I were you,' says the little boy. 'Mammy will go mad. There's only one potty under the bed and at the moment I'm using it.'

Three little boys went into a sweet shop. The first boy asked for ten pence worth of apple drops, which just happened to be on the top shelf. The elderly shop-keeper went to the back of the shop, got the ladder, settled it, climbed up, got the jar down and weighed out ten pence worth of apple drops. Then he returned the ladder to the back of the shop.

'Now, what would you like?' he asked the second little boy.

'I'd like ten pence worth of apple drops as well please.'

So the shopkeeper went to the back of the shop again to get his ladder. He returned, settled it, climbed up, got the jar down and gave the little boy ten pence worth of apple drops.

Then he turned to the third boy and says, 'Would you like ten pence worth of apple drops as well?'

'No, thank you,' says the boy.

So the elderly shopkeeper returned the ladder to the back of the shop, came back and, gasping, says to the third little boy, 'Now, what would you like?'

'I'd like twenty pence worth of apple drops, please.'

An official from the Department of Agriculture was visiting a farm in Wicklow one day, and was amazed to see a pig walking around the farm with a wooden leg. So he decided to ask the farmer about it.

'Oh, that pig really is the most wonderful pig that ever lived,' says the proud farmer. 'One day I was doing some work in the barn beyond when I dozed off. While I was asleep, a spark from the chimney in the house set the barn ablaze. Do you know, that pig there broke out of his pen and fought his way through the flames to drag me out to safety with his teeth. As a matter of fact, I feel I owe my life to that pig.'

'That's a pretty amazing story,' says the official. 'But you still haven't told me why it's got a wooden leg.'

'Well, a wonderful pig like that,' says the farmer, 'you couldn't just eat it all at once.'

A man is selling flowers in Grafton Street one day, when a businessman passes by.

'How about a bunch of flowers for the wife?'

'I don't have a wife,' came the gruff reply.

'Well, how about a bunch for your girlfriend?' the flower-seller says persuasively.

'I don't have a girlfriend either,' says the business-man.

'You're a very lucky man,' says the flower-seller. 'Buy a couple of bunches to celebrate.'

Two Dublin women were really looking forward to their trip to the Algarve.

They had never been away before, and were enjoying their chat on the plane.

One of them looked out the cabin window and says, 'My God! Just look at all those people down there. It's amazing, they look just like ants!'

Her friend leaned across and says, 'You stupid idiot. They *are* ants. We haven't taken off yet.'

Maurice's mother-in-law called over one evening, looking a lot better than she normally did.

'So you've been to the beauty parlour, then,' says Maurice.

'Beauty parlour my arse,' says the mother-in-law. 'I've just been run over by a bus.'

An elderly Cork lady was on her first visit to Dublin and decided to pay a visit to Dublin Zoo. On her way in she bought several packets of peanuts and headed straight for the monkey cage.

To her bitter disappointment, there wasn't a monkey to be seen.

She spotted one of the keepers and called him over to register her complaint.

'Well, madam,' says the keeper, 'it's like this. It's the, eh, mating season, you know. And all the monkeys are around the back, eh, making ... love ... you know yourself.'

'Do you think they'd come out for a few peanuts?' asked the old lady.

'Would you?' replied the keeper.

Father Ryan was a very keen fisherman.

One morning he was all set for a good day's fishing, when he was suddenly asked to perform a wedding for a local couple.

Two minutes into the ceremony he hurriedly asked the bride, 'Look, do you promise to love, honour and obey this man?'

'I do,' came the reply.

'Fair enough,' says Father Ryan. 'Reel him in.'

It was Maurice's first day on the building site, and he was enjoying a cup of tea with the foreman during the morning break.

'I can't understand why they erected statues on this type of building,' says Maurice.

'They're not statues,' says the foreman, 'they're bricklayers.'

'My mother-in-law has disappeared.'

'Have you given her description to the police?'

'No. They'd never believe me.'

Trainer to jockey: 'Couldn't you have gone any faster?'

Jockey: 'Yes, but the rules say that I must stay with the horse.'

Noah was watching his sons fishing from the Ark one day and shouted over to them, 'Go easy on the maggots, lads. I've only got the two.'

A Russian and an Irishman were deeply engrossed in a very serious chess game.

For a long time neither of them moved, but after seven hours' solid playing, the Russian became restless.

The Irishman turned to him and says, 'That's the second time you've moved since we sat down. Are you playing chess or dancing?'

Teacher: 'Now, Joe, if one and one make two, and two and two make four, what do four and four make?'

Joe: 'How come you always answer the easy ones yourself and ask me the hard ones?'

Paddy broke into Number 10 Downing Street, and ten minutes later he was caught by the police.

'Paddy Murphy, you are under arrest for breaking into the home of the prime minister.'

'Fair enough,' says Paddy, realising the game was up. 'But my God, how the hell did you catch me so quickly?'

'Well,' says the policeman, 'you shouldn't have signed the visitors' book.'

An old farmer was a bit worried about his favourite bull. It was ignoring all the cows.

So he went to the local vet, who gave him some medicine. The next day he was telling one of his neighbours about it. 'You know,' he says, 'I gave that bull of mine just one dose of that concoction, and within an hour he'd serviced nine cows.'

'That's amazing,' says the neighbour. 'What's the stuff called?'

'Well,' says the farmer, 'the label's come off the bottle, but it tastes a bit like peppermint.'

Maurice and Vera were going through a bad patch, so they decided to see a marriage counsellor.

While they were sitting in the waiting room, Vera gave Maurice the hawk-eye and says, 'Now, remember, when he starts to talk about how neither of us should dominate the other, you keep your big mouth shut!'

An old man went to see his doctor after he developed a urinary problem.

'Doctor,' he says, 'I can't urinate.'

The doctor took one look at him and says, 'Mr O'Reilly, you're eighty-four years of age. You've urinated enough.'

A man was suing Dublin Corporation. Eventually his case was settled and he called to his solicitor's office to pick up his cheque.

'Hold on a minute!' he says to his solicitor. 'This is only a third of the full amount I was awarded!'

'That is correct,' says the solicitor. 'I took the rest.'

'You!' shouted the man. 'I was the one who was injured!'

'I understand,' says the solicitor, 'but you seem to forget that I was the one who built up the case. I provided the intelligence necessary to proceed and convince the jury, and it was I who presented your case in a way that the judge praised and recommended should be recorded in the Law Library. Any idiot can fall down a manhole.'

Ronan and Des approached the first tee for their annual game of golf. Both men were good players, each was determined to win, and back in the clubhouse the betting was heavy. Ronan was keenly aware of Des's little ploy, of breaking wind just as his opponent was about to play a shot, particularly a match-winning shot.

They had a very competitive game, and Des lived up to his nickname of Windcheater.

Finally they reached the eighteenth hole and Ronan had to sink a three-foot putt to win. He got down on one knee, examined the line, felt the grass, rubbed his putter, took his stance, shuffled his feet into position and played the ball. It trickled along and stopped about an inch from the hole.

'Dammit!' Ronan shouted at Des. 'That's all your fault, you and your bloody farting!'

'But I didn't fart,' says Des, 'I swear.'

'No, I know you didn't,' says Ronan, 'but I allowed for it.'

A man comes up to me in the street one day and says, 'I haven't had a bite in three days.'

So I bit him.

Short-sighted Mrs Murphy was sick in bed and received a visit from, as she thought, the local parish priest.

After he had left, she told her son-in-law how much she appreciated the priest calling to see her.

'But, Mother,' says the son-in-law, 'that wasn't the priest, that was the doctor.'

'It's funny you should mention that,' says the old lady. 'I thought Father Mulligan was being a bit familiar.'

A drunk was on a bus, tearing up a newspaper into small pieces and throwing them out the window.

The man sitting next to him was becoming irritated, and says, 'What the hell are you doing, tearing up that paper and throwing it out the window like that?'

'Scaring away the elephants,' says the drunk.

'But there are no elephants on the bus,' says the man.

'I know,' the drunk slurred. 'It's very effective, isn't it?'

Barman on the telephone: 'Madam, I'm afraid this bar is packed with low-down, good-for-nothing, lazy, drunken, up-all-nighter husbands. You're going to have to give me a better description than that.'

A man had a very bad attack of that universal complaint, piles.

The doctor examined his backside and said that where modern medicine offered no solution, he would like to try a possible new cure a local gypsy had told him about.

The man agreed and the doctor put a load of tea-leaves in the appropriate place, mentioning that the cure would take about two weeks to have an effect.

After a week the pain was so bad that the man decided that this old-fashioned cure wasn't working and he went to visit a different doctor.

The man explained what was wrong, and the doctor asked him to bend over for an examination.

'Well,' says the doctor, 'I'm afraid the only thing I can do for you is to give you some ointment. But to be honest, I can see your piles and they look nasty.'

'Can you see anything else?' enquired the patient.

'I can,' says the doctor. 'I see a tall dark stranger and you are going on a very long journey with a beautiful lady.'

An elderly truck driver was sitting in a roadside café, when ten burly Hell's Angels came barging in. They started to take over the place, cursing and shouting as they caused havoc. After a few minutes they started to pick on the old lorry driver. He kept his cool and didn't react when they poured coffee all over him. Even when they put their cigarettes out on his plate of egg and chips, he didn't blink an eyelid. He just sat there, close to tears, without offering any resistance. Finally he got up, paid the girl behind the counter and headed for his truck.

One of the Hell's Angels turned to the girl and says, 'Not much of a man, is he?'

'No,' says the girl, looking out the window. 'And he's not much of a driver either. He's just backed his lorry over ten motorbikes.'

A man walks into a chip shop, orders a fish and chip, and is promptly served.

Five minutes later he returns in an angry mood.

'Excuse me,' he shouts, demanding the assistant's attention. 'Are you sure that fish was cooked properly?'

'Why?' asks the curious assistant.

'Because it's just eaten all my bloody chips.'

An American tourist was driving through Cork one day and as he was passing through a small village, he saw a young man running very fast with three ferocious, mad-looking dogs close behind him.

The tourist pulled over and, opening the door, shouted, 'Get in quick.'

'Thanks a million,' says the man. 'Most people won't give me a lift when they see I have three dogs with me.'

A man has been with his new employer for only a fortnight but decides he should be getting a better pay deal. So he goes to see the boss.

'My God, I don't believe this!' says the boss. 'You're only with us two weeks and already you expect an increase. Surely you know that you have to work yourself up.'

'Work myself up?' says the employee. 'Work myself up? My bloody nerves are gone.'

A little boy found a bullet in the street and swallowed it. When his mother found out what had happened, she rushed him to the local doctor in a panic. The doctor spent three hours examining the little boy and eventually he called the mother in.

'Your son will be fine,' the doctor says reassuringly. 'Take him home now and give him a good pint of castor oil.'

'But, doctor,' says the woman, 'a pint of castor oil? Wouldn't that be dangerous?'

'Not at all,' says the doc. 'Just don't point him at anyone.'

Paddy's mother-in-law was working on the farm one day when his mule suddenly attacked her. She died instantly.

There was a huge turn-out at the funeral. About seven hundred, mostly men. After the funeral the parish priest says to Paddy, 'Isn't that a lovely tribute? I never realised how popular your mother-in-law was. Just imagine seven hundred here for the funeral.'

Paddy says, 'They're not here for the funeral, Father, they're here to buy the mule.'

I was down at my local one day and I bumped into a friend whose mother-in-law had just died. I offered my condolences: 'It must be very hard to lose a mother-in-law.'

'Hard?' he says. 'It's almost impossible.'

This guy sees an ad in the newspaper for a holiday to America for £15 return. He's thinking to himself this must be some mistake but decides to follow it up. So he goes to the agency, which is down a little side street, and knocks on the door.

The door opens and someone comes out and gives him a smack with a cosh.

Next thing he knows, he wakes up and he's strapped to an oar with fifty others, and there's this guy shackled beside him with a long beard and ragged clothes, and another guy walking up and down cracking a bullwhip and shouting, 'Row, you wasters, row!'

He turns to the guy with the beard and says, 'This is crazy. I thought I was going on a luxury cruise for £15. Do they at least take you back home?'

'Well,' says your man, 'they didn't last year.'

A doctor was sitting in his office when he noticed his sink was leaking. He tried to fix it but couldn't, so he called a plumber.

The plumber arrived, got stuck in and had the job done before too long. He then handed the doctor a bill for £200.

The doctor took one look at the bill and says, 'Two hundred pounds! That's scandalous. You were here less than an hour. I'm a top doctor, and even I don't get two hundred pounds an hour.'

'I know,' says the plumber sympathetically. 'When I was a doctor I didn't either.'

A salesman was travelling from Dublin to Cork when he stopped in the midlands to answer a call of nature. Just as he was getting out of the car, he was attacked and beaten up by a gang of fellas. They robbed his wallet and left him dazed on the ground.

Some time later a garda car found him by the roadside.

'What happened?' asked one of the guards.

'Well,' says the man, 'just as I was getting out of my car, they came at me from behind and struck me over the head with a sack of apples.'

'Do you think you'd recognise them if you saw them?' enquired the second guard.

'I certainly would,' replied the man. 'They were Granny Smiths.'

An enormously fat lady got on a bus in O'Connell Street. The bus was very full (even the driver was standing). She hung on to a strap and glared round the bus at the other passengers, most of whom were men.

'Isn't anyone going to offer me a seat?' she growled.

At this a man got up and says, 'Well, I'm willing to make a small contribution.'

Larry, a popular waiter, has died. When his regular diners hear about his death, they decide to try and contact him through a medium. So they find a medium and they all gather at a table in Larry's old restaurant after hours.

The medium tells them all to join hands and chant his name over and over again. So they join hands and, on the count of three, begin chanting, 'Larry, Larry, Larry.'

Nothing. Silence. So they try it again. There's still no word from the deceased waiter.

So they try once more, a little louder, and lo and behold, Larry appears hovering above their heads.

'Larry,' one of the customers says, 'it's terrific to see you, really terrific, but tell me, why did we have to call you three times?'

'Bloody right you had to wait,' says Larry. 'I'm not looking after this table.'

Clairvoyant: 'I see a very short life ahead for you, Mrs Jones. Mrs Jones . . . Mrs Jones!'

Maurice says to his mother-in-law one night in the pub over a few drinks, 'My house is your house. My land is your land. I just want you to know that.'

Two weeks later she sold it!

When Maurice was going to America on holiday some years ago, he was stopped at the immigration section at JFK Airport.

The customs official took a good long hard look at him and asked him if he was a natural-born Irish citizen.

'Oh no,' says Maurice, 'I was born Caesarean.'

The Hunchback of Notre Dame wasn't very happy with his lot, so he went to see the boss.

'I've been here for almost forty years now,' he began, 'and to be perfectly honest, I don't think I'm getting the kind of money that I should be getting. Why only yesterday I was reading in the *Notre Dame News* that someone with my qualifications should be entitled to back money.'

'I agree entirely,' says the boss. 'Would a lump sum be OK?'

A cannibal goes on holiday to Majorca. When he returns home he only has one leg.

It was self-catering!

A man had his fingers cut off both hands in an accident at the sawmill. He was rushed to hospital.

He was on the operating table, obviously in great pain and distress, so the surgeon says to him, 'Don't be worrying now, Mr Mooney, we can do wonders nowadays. What with plastic surgery and micro-lasers, we'll have your fingers sewn back on and working in no time. By the way, you did bring your fingers with you, didn't you?'

'I'm afraid not,' says Mr Mooney. 'I couldn't pick them up.'

The doctor's phone rang in the middle of the night.

'Doctor, this is Mr Jones, 74 Railway Street. My wife has terrible pains and I was wondering if you could come and see her straight away. She's in agony. I think it might be appendicitis.'

'That's impossible,' says the doctor. 'Your wife had her appendix out twenty years ago. Have you ever heard of anyone having a second appendix?'

'No, doctor,' says Mr Jones, 'I haven't, but have you ever heard of anyone having a second wife?'

Two guys are sitting in their office one day, when suddenly a brick smashes through the window, with a note attached to it: 'John Murphy and Sons, Hammond Lane. Glass cut to all sizes.'

'Do you know where that place is?' says one of the men.

'I do,' says the other. 'It's only a stone's throw away.'

Two Jews, Hymie a...
night. Halfway th...
making funny no...

'Are you OK...

'I . . . I . . . t...

Hymie, strug...

'Are you...

'No,' says...

Letter to the editor
Dear Sir
As a Scotsm...
years, I resen...
my fellow...
Furtherm...
that, I...
your...

A woman goes to see her dentist, ... obviously very nervous. 'God,' she says, ... which I'd prefer, having a tooth out or having a...

'Well,' says the dentist, 'will you make up your mind, because I'll have to adjust the chair.'

An old maid ran into a garda station shouting, 'Help, help!'

A garda calmed her down and told her to take a seat.

'Now,' he began, 'tell me what's wrong.'

'Well,' says the woman, 'I was walking in the park across the road when a young man made some very indecent proposals to me.'

'When exactly did this happen?' asked the guard.

'About twenty years ago,' says the old woman.

'And why are you telling us about it now?' enquired the guard.

'Oh, I just like talking about it,' says the woman.

n living in Dublin for the past twenty
very much your recent article typifying
ountrymen as being mean and thrifty.
re, if you continue to publish articles like
ll have no alternative but to stop borrowing
aper from my next door neighbour.
ours etc.
Ben Down

Did you hear about the two nudists who were going out together? They broke it off because they were seeing too much of each other.

A Dublin couple were up in the zoo one day, enjoying their visit. As they were walking past the monkey house, a huge gorilla suddenly jumped out of nowhere and started ripping all the woman's clothes off.

'Jesus, Mary and Holy St Joseph, Des! What will I do?'

'Do what you always do,' says her husband. 'Tell him you have a headache.'

An elderly man goes into a record shop and calls the female assistant.

'You have an album in the window there called *Music For Pleasure*. How much is it?'

'It's nine pounds,' says the girl.

'Well forget about the music,' says the old man. 'How much is it just for the pleasure?'

An American tourist and his wife were on holiday in Killarney. While out touring one day, they came across a wishing well. They both tossed in a coin and were engrossed in their own private thoughts. The wife leaned over to look down the deep well but suddenly lost her balance and fell to the bottom, hundreds of feet below.

'Well, Holy God,' says the husband. 'These things really do work!'

Two down-on-their-luck actors meet in the street one day.

'I hear you've just landed a part,' says Nigel.

'Yes, I have,' replies Norman. 'I'm going to play Long John Silver.'

'How much are they paying you?' asks Nigel.

'Three thousand pounds a week,' says Norman.

'And when do you start?'

'Next Monday.'

'Next Monday? Why, for that kind of money I'd start tomorrow.'

'I can't do that,' says Norman. 'I'm having my leg off.'

Pat called to see his friend Mick one day, and found him in a very distressed state.

'My God,' says Pat, 'what's wrong?'

'I've been trying to commit suicide,' says Mick, his face very pale.

'Well, if you're going to do it, why not put that rope there around your neck?'

'Oh, I tried that,' says Mick, 'but the bloody thing nearly choked me.'

During his last years, Leonid Brezhnev, the Russian leader, was suddenly rushed to a Moscow hospital for emergency surgery.

One of his bodyguards from the KGB approached the surgeon in a state of panic and sobbed, 'Is this it, doctor? Is our great leader dying?'

'Not at all,' says the doctor. 'We just have to widen his rib-cage to make room for more medals.'

Two fortune-tellers met in the street one day.

'Beautiful weather we're having, isn't it?' one says to the other.

'It certainly is,' came the reply. 'Reminds me of the great summer of 2010.'

A little boy goes into Uncle George's pet shop in Dublin and says to the assistant, 'Have yiz any wasps?'

'No, we've no wasps,' came the reply. The little boy turned and walked out.

Twenty minutes later he returned and again asked the assistant, 'Have yiz any wasps?'

'Listen, I've told you already, we've no wasps,' the assistant says angrily. Again the boy turned and left the store without a word.

Ten minutes later he was back. 'Excuse me,' he says, 'but have yiz any wasps?'

'Listen, you little troublemaker,' shouted the assistant, 'I've told you once, I've told you twice, and I won't tell you again. Now read my lips. We have no bloody wasps.'

'Well, that's funny,' says the kid. 'Yiz had one in the window yesterday.'

Paddy Murphy arrived at the gates of heaven.

'Where are you from?' asked St Peter.

'I'm from Ireland,' Paddy says proudly.

'Well, you can bugger off,' says St Peter. 'There's no way I'm doing Irish stew for one.'

There was an accident on a building site in London and poor Murphy lay dead on the ground. The foreman was panic-stricken and gathered his men together.

'Look, lads,' he says, 'I'm a bit worried that the media are going to get hold of this story and poor Mick's family will hear it from them first. I'd prefer if his wife heard it from one of us. Now, does anyone know where he lived?'

Tom Doolan put up his hand and says, 'I do, boss. Would you like me to go?'

'Be God, that would be great,' says the foreman. 'Now, whatever you do, make sure you break it to his wife gently.'

'I certainly will,' says Doolan, and he was off.

Ten minutes later he knocked on the door and a lady answered.

'Are you the Widow Murphy?' he asked.

'I am not,' says the woman.

'You wanna bet?' says Doolan.

An American tourist checked into his hotel in Galway. As he was unpacking he noticed some things on the bedside locker. There was a Bible, a notepad and pencil and a little card that read, 'Are you an alcoholic? Do you have a problem with drink? If so, please call 52537.'

So he did. It was an off-licence!

A man goes into a garage in Dublin and says to the salesman, 'Excuse me, but do you remember selling me a 1984 Fiat Ritmo about three weeks ago?'

'I do indeed, sir,' says the salesman.

'Well,' says your man, 'would you mind telling me all about how good it is again, because I'm getting very discouraged.'

QUICKIES

Did you hear about the RTÉ musician who spent three weeks working on an arrangement, and then his wife didn't go away after all!

I was in a taxi last night. The meter was going faster than the car.

He's a great swimmer. He can swim one hundred yards in four seconds. Mind you, that's going over a waterfall.

Women. They make up their faces quicker than they make up their minds.

He who laughs last ... usually has a tooth missing.

She was a straight actress. Her figure was 34-34-34.

She had a lot of funny lines. All in her face.

There's no place quite like Venice. The only city where you can get seasick crossing the road.

His brother is with the special branch. They finally caught up with him.

She has a figure like the Supreme Court. No appeal.

She's been stood up more times than a bowling pin.

It pays to stand up for your rights. But not in the middle of the M50.

The only time people look like their passport photo is during a hijacking.

They say Adam was the luckiest man in history – no mother-in-law. That's why it was called paradise.

He's so dumb he thought Yoko Ono was the Japanese for 'one egg'.

She had teeth like the Ten Commandments – all broken.

I've been at some football games that were terrible. Even the band played better than the teams.

Is he ugly? I'll put it like this, Hallowe'en is the only time he can go out without a mask.

Did you know we only use 20 per cent of our brainpower. Apparently the other 70 per cent just lies dormant.

I'm not saying she's a big girl, but when he carried her over the threshold he had to make three trips.

He's a real loner. He plays strip solitaire.

As a couple, they don't get on very well. In fact, the last time they held hands was at a séance.

We used to call him Surrender. One look at him and you give up.

He's very highly strung – but not high enough.

She was nearly four hours in the beauty salon – and that was just getting an estimate.

Holiday charter flights are so crowded these days! The last flight I was on, the plane was so overcrowded the pilot had to go by boat.

He bought a book called *How To Be the Boss in Your Own Home* but his wife wouldn't let him read it.

Maurice has just got one of those new seat-belts for his car. One part of the strap goes across Vera's waist, and the other part goes across her mouth.

He went to see *Jaws* and asked for a seat in the shallow end.

He went to see a movie called *The Desert* and asked for two seats in the shade.

She's a very jealous person. She even had male bridesmaids.

It takes her an hour to cook Uncle Ben's Five-Minute Rice.

I always know when she's doing a salad – I can't smell anything burning.

If you were married to my wife you'd understand why we pray before each meal.

She brings more bills into the house than Tony Gregory.

All the time he was in the army his wife sent him nagging letters. He couldn't even enjoy the war in peace.

For his birthday I wanted to give him something he really needed. But how do you wrap up a bath?

Is he ugly? He looks like his hobby is stepping on rakes. He looks like his face went on fire and someone tried to put it out with a shovel.

I come from a very large family. At Christmas my mother used to get a twenty-eight-pound turkey.
   She had to get an upholsterer to stuff it.

The supermarket – a place where you can spend half an hour looking for instant coffee.

According to a recent survey, married men live longer than single men. It's not true.

It just seems longer.

He married her for her looks – but not the kind he gets from her now.

He drank an awful lot. He died on a Thursday. His liver didn't die until the following Tuesday. They had to beat it to death with a stick.

When he was having his photograph taken, the photographer told him to act natural.

So he started filling his pockets with rolls of film and stuff.

In one race the horse was so slow, the jockey kept a diary of the trip.

Does he eat a lot? That fella would eat a picture of the Last Supper.

How to turn your mother-in-law into an Olympic runner. First you get a Rottweiler dog . . .

He was out with twins last night. I says to him, 'Did you have a good time?'

He says, 'Well, yes and no.'

I just got this new fire and theft policy from my insurance company, and to be honest I'm a bit worried about it. They only pay out if my house is broken into while it's on fire!

I went to see the acupuncturist. It was very quiet ... you could hear a pin drop.

I'm not saying my wife spends a lot on clothes, but A-Wear have just opened a branch in our living-room.

Two Irish guys were shipwrecked on a desert island. One day a boat drifted up on the beach, so they broke it up and made a raft.

I'm not saying the smog in Dublin is bad, but I was in O'Connell Street the other day and I'm sure I saw the statue of James Larkin coughing.

NOT WELCOME

When calling to a 'friend's' house, you know you're not welcome when...

The whole family open the door and say, 'Yeah?'

A bucket of hot tar is thrown from the top window.

The house you're calling on has central locking.

The bell is disconnected and the knocker has been removed.

The welcome mat reads 'Bugger off'.

You can clearly hear the entire family rushing out the back door.

STRANGE BUT TRUE

Did you hear about the Irish astronomer who got fired because he wouldn't work nights?

Did you know that the man who invented slow-motion movies got the idea while watching a Scotsman reaching for his wallet in a restaurant?

In India on a certain feast day they actually roast an elephant.

It takes twenty-eight men to pull the wishbone.

In a survey, 28 per cent of American men said they would be willing to have sex for money. 72 per cent said they'd do it for nothing.

A man phones his doctor.

'Ah, Mr Smith, how can I help you?'

'Well, doctor, it's my wife. She's just dislocated her jaw and I was wondering if you could possibly pop over in say ... three or four weeks?'

What part of your body shouldn't move when you're dancing?

Your bowels!

We were playing Trivial Pursuit last night, and Maurice ate three of the questions. He thought they were After Eights.

Boy, is she house-proud. She has more disinfectant in the house than they used in the Second World War.

'Doctor, I keep thinking I'm a car.'

'Well, just pull in over there.'

After a lovely meal in a restaurant, Maurice says to the waiter, 'Will you put that bit of chicken I didn't eat into a bag for the dog. And would you mind throwing in a couple of slices of bread as well in case he fancies a sandwich.'

The food in the restaurant was so bad that on the other side of the menu there was a list of doctors on call.

A union official is tucking his child in to bed with a bedtime story. He begins, 'Once upon a time-and-a-half . . .'

His problem is basically concentration. The only time he can keep his mind on two things at the same time is when he's at a Dolly Parton concert.

He's turned a few heads in his time. Mind you, he's turned a few stomachs as well!

At the Christmas party the office Romeo approached one of the girls with a drink.

'Here you go,' he says, 'Scotch and a chaser.'

'Where's the chaser?' she asked.

'You're looking at him.'

AND FINALLY . . .

An old man turned up at a lumberjacks' camp in Wicklow one day, looking for work.

None of the men would take him seriously but he begged to show them what he could do.

Eventually, just to humour him, the boss agreed and, handing him an axe, says, 'Now take it easy, old fella, we don't want you killing yourself.'

The old man took the axe and headed straight for the largest, thickest tree in the forest. He started chopping furiously and within three minutes the tree was lying on the ground. The other lumberjacks stood there open-mouthed.

'That's amazing,' says the boss. 'Where did you learn to chop trees like that?'

'Well,' says the man, 'I received my basic training in the Sahara.'

'But . . . but . . . ' stuttered the boss, 'there are no trees in the Sahara. It's a desert.'

The old man winked at him and says, 'It is now.'

86

A Dublin taxi driver is asked by an American tourist to show him the sights of the city. So they head off first to the Phoenix Park.

'Call that a park?' says the loud-mouthed tourist. 'Why, my front lawn is bigger than that.'

The taxi driver just shrugs his shoulders and drives on, this time stopping at the GPO in O'Connell Street.

'Call that a post office?' says the Yank. 'My garden shed is twice that size.'

The driver remains silent and motors on towards Blessington Lakes.

'A lake?' the tourist screams with laughter. 'Why, my garden pond is bigger than that.'

The driver just raises his eyes and says nothing. Just as he is pulling away from the lakes, three donkeys block his path. He rolls his window down and, shooing them away, turns to the American tourist, raises his eyes and sighs, 'Bloody rabbits.'

A lady buys a new car and is driving it home for the first time when she notices that no matter what she does, she can't get the radio to work. So she heads straight back to the garage.

'I'm so sorry,' says the salesman. 'I did mean to explain that this is a new concept car, and your radio works only on your voice commands. I do apologise. Now let me explain. If you want classical music while you're driving, all you have to do is say "classical music" and the radio will search out and play whichever station is playing classical music. On the other hand, if your preference is country and western, simply say "country and western" and your radio will do all the work. It never fails.'

The lady is delighted with her new system and heads off home. On her way she decides to try it out.

'Rock-and-roll,' she says, and on comes Chuck Berry.

'Country and western,' she says, delighted with herself, and in the blink of an eye John Denver is singing on her radio.

'Classical music,' she shouts, obviously warming to this great new idea, and true enough, the soothing sounds of Bach emerge. Just as she is enjoying the lovely warm sound, a trucker overtakes her at fierce speed, almost sending her new car flying into a ditch.

'Arsehole,' she shouts, and a voice comes on the radio: 'Good morning, this is Gerry Ryan.'